I Know My Savior Lives

A Year of Prepared Family Night Lessons
and Activities to Strengthen Your Home

KIMIKO CHRISTENSEN HAMMARI

CFI
An Imprint of Cedar Fort, Inc.
Springville, Utah

For Dan,
who always shows me Christlike love.

ISBN 13: 978-1-4621-1471-9

Published by CFI, an imprint of Cedar Fort, Inc.
2373 W. 700 S., Springville, UT, 84663
Distributed by Cedar Fort, Inc., www.cedarfort.com

Library of Congress Control Number: 2014951414

Cover design by Shawnda Craig
Cover design © 2014 by Lyle Mortimer
Edited by Kevin Haws

Printed in the United States of America

10 9 8 7 6 5 4 3 2 1

Printed on acid-free paper

Contents

How to Use This Book

This book provides a year's worth of family home evening lessons that teach your children about the Savior. In order to get the most out of this manual and reinforce what your children are learning in Primary, teach the lessons in order.

The lessons are divided into monthly themes and subdivided into weekly themes. Four lessons are provided for most months. However, in some months, there are only three. In those cases use the extra week to review what you learned previously, or use it for those special Monday nights when family home evening is in a different form (such as a school event that can't be missed or an extended family activity).

Each lesson is divided into the following sections:

Resources

Scriptures, Primary songs, hymns, and pictures from the *Gospel Art Book*.

(Note: The *Gospel Art Book* is available at www.lds.org. You can download and print pictures or show the pictures to your children on the computer if Interent access is available during your lesson. You can order a copy of the *Gospel Art Book* at store.lds.org.)

Lesson

A brief explanation of the theme is given with corresponding scriptures and discussion questions.

Activity

The activities are meant to reinforce what is taught in the lesson, so they may not be the games your family is used to playing. Most lessons include separate activities for younger children and older children. Generally, the activities for younger children are for ages three to seven, and those activities for older children, eight to eleven. However, don't use this guideline as a firm rule. Some younger children may be advanced for their age, and some older children may still enjoy the activities for younger children. You know your children best, so use the activities that you think they will enjoy.

Challenge

These challenges should be completed during the week before the next Monday. At the beginning of each family home evening, follow up with your children on the previous week's challenge. Discuss their success and help them with any problems or concerns.

Each lesson includes a challenge card that should be printed from the included CD. Your children should fill out a card and put it somewhere they will see it during the week so they can be reminded of what to work on. The challenge cards include a line where your children can sign their names and formally commit to the challenge. This method will help your children understand that writing down a goal makes it a more solid commitment.

CD-ROM

The CD has been provided for your convenience in printing handouts, challenge cards, and other lesson materials. This entire book is available on the CD and can be printed in color. It is recommended that you print out activities and challenge cards from the CD so you don't have to write in your book or cut it up. A "Read Me" file on the CD explains how to use it.

January

We Believe in God, the Eternal
Father, and in His Son, Jesus Christ

God is the Father of my spirit.

Resources

(Select one from each category.)

Children's Songbook
+ I Lived in Heaven (4)
+ My Heavenly Father Loves Me (228)

Hymn
+ I Am a Child of God (301)
+ I Know My Father Lives (302)

Scriptures
+ Galatians 4:7
+ 1 John 3:2

Lesson

God is the Father of our spirits. Before we came to earth, we lived as spirit children with Heavenly Father. He knew and loved us, just as He does now. We are literally children of God. Though we have parents here on earth, Heavenly Father will always be the Father of our spirits. We cannot see Him, but He will always look out for us, just as our earthly parents do. He wants us to be happy and return to Him someday. He wants to bless us and give us all the wonderful things He has.

Read and discuss Romans 8:16–17.

+ What is an heir? What does it mean to be joint-heirs with Christ?
+ Why does Heavenly Father want to share His glory with us?

Activity

Younger Children: See page 4.

Older Children: God is the Father of your spirit, and you have many unique traits. Look through magazines and cut out pictures that represent you and your interests. Glue the pictures on a piece of paper and make a collage. At the top, write your name and the phrase "I Am a Child of God." You can use the template on page 5 or design your own.

Challenge

Heavenly Father loves you and wants to hear from you often. Even though you can't see Him, you can pray to Him. Set a goal this week to make your daily prayers more sincere so your relationship with Him will grow. Express gratitude for your blessings, tell Him about the good things that happen to you, tell Him about your problems, and ask Him for help.

Challenge

This week, I commit to make my prayers to Heavenly Father more sincere. I will express my gratitude, tell Him about my day, and ask for help when I need it.

_____
Signature

_____
Date

I Am a Child of God

We are all children of God, no matter where we were born or what we look like. Below is a picture of children from different parts of the world. Draw a picture of yourself with these children.

I Am a Child of God

_____
Name

Jesus Christ is the Son of God.

Resources

(Select one from each category.)

Children's Songbook
- I Lived in Heaven (4)
- God's Love (97)

Hymn
- I Am a Child of God (301)
- I Know My Father Lives (302)

Gospel Art Book
- Jesus Christ (1)
- The Birth of Jesus Christ (30)

Scriptures
- Psalm 82:6
- Galatians 4:7
- 1 John 3:2

Lesson

Jesus is more than a good man, and even greater than a prophet. Jesus Christ is the Son of God. God is our Heavenly Father (the Father of our spirits), and we each have an earthly father as well. But Jesus is different. God was both Jesus's Heavenly Father and earthly father. Jesus was God's firstborn son in the premortal world, and He had a very special mission to fulfill here on earth. God chose Jesus to be our Savior because He knew Jesus would be obedient.

Jesus always obeyed His Father. He was tempted and faced hard times, just like we do. However, Jesus understood who He was and knew that He had a divine mission to fulfill. Because He loved Heavenly Father so much, He kept the commandments and endured to the end. He is a great example to us.

Read and discuss Matthew 16:13–17.
- Why do you think some people disagree on who Jesus was?
- How did Peter gain his testimony that Jesus was the Son of God? How can we gain our own testimonies?

Activity

Younger Children: Color the picture on page 8.
Older Children: See page 9.

Challenge

Learn three names that Jesus Christ is called by. **You can use the list on page 9** or look in the Topical Guide. Find out why Jesus is known by each name. You can ask your parents or primary teacher, or find the answers yourself in the scriptures.

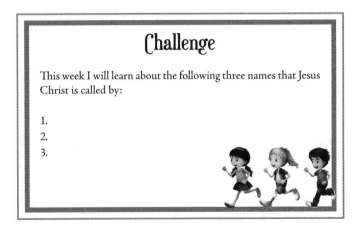

Challenge

This week I will learn about the following three names that Jesus Christ is called by:

1.
2.
3.

Jesus Christ is the Son of God

Hangman

Use some of the words below to play Hangman with your family. Each completed puzzle will reveal one of the names of the Savior. Use a chalkboard or dry erase board so everyone can see. A large piece of paper will also work.

ADVOCATE
ALMIGHTY
BELOVED
BREAD OF LIFE
CHRIST
CREATOR
EMMANUEL
EXEMPLAR
GOD OF ISRAEL
JEHOVAH
LAMB OF GOD
LORD
MAKER
MASTER
MESSIAH
ONLY BEGOTTEN
REDEEMER
SON

Resources

(Select one from each category.)

Children's Songbook
- Jesus Is Our Loving Friend (58b)
- Jesus Loved the Little Children (59)
- My Heavenly Father Loves Me (228)

Hymn
- God Is Love (87)
- Our Savior's Love (113)

Gospel Art Book
- Christ and the Children (47)
- Jesus Carrying a Lost Lamb (64)

Scriptures
- 1 Nephi 11:17
- 1 John 4:7–8

Heavenly Father and Jesus Christ love me.

Lesson

Heavenly Father and Jesus Christ love us very much. It doesn't matter that we aren't perfect. It doesn't matter that we are all different—that some of us are short, some are tall, some are thin, some are round, some have curly hair, some have straight hair. To them, each of us is worth far more than gold. Sometimes we are sad and feel all alone. Sometimes we may feel that no one understands us. But always remember how much Heavenly Father and Jesus Christ love you. Their love for you will never change, no matter what. They will always be there for you.

Read and discuss Romans 8:23–39.

- What are some of the things mentioned in these verses that can separate us from the love of Heavenly Father and Jesus Christ? Is there anything else that can separate us from their love?

- What are some of the ways Heavenly Father shows you He loves you?

Activity

Younger Children: Color the picture on page 12.

Older Children: Cut out the hearts on page 13. (Color them first if you wish.) On each heart, write something that helps you remember that Heavenly Father and Jesus love you. It could be your family, the beautiful tree in your yard, a blessing you received—pretty much anything. Hang the hearts in different places around the house to remind you that Heavenly Father and Jesus love you.

Challenge

Every day for the next week, write down one of the things you notice that shows God loves you. Record it on your gratitude poster, if you have one.

Challenge

Each day this week, I will write down one of the things I notice that shows Heavenly Father and Jesus Christ love me.

_____

Signature

_____

Date

Jesus loves the little children

February

Jesus Christ Is My Savior and Redeemer

Jesus Christ is my Savior and Redeemer.

Lesson

When Heavenly Father presented His plan to us, we were excited and shouted with joy. But we knew, and Heavenly Father knew, we could not complete our life on earth alone. No matter how hard we tried to keep the commandments, we would still make mistakes. We needed a Savior, someone who would save us from our sins.

Jesus Christ and Lucifer both offered to be our Savior. Lucifer wanted to force us to keep all the commandments, and he wanted to receive all the glory for it. Jesus, on the other hand, said he would let us grow by making our own choices. He would give His life for us in order to redeem us from our sins, and the glory would be His Father's. Heavenly Father chose Jesus to be our Savior and Redeemer.

Because Jesus gave His life for us, we have the freedom to choose right from wrong. When we make a mistake, we can repent and be forgiven. And if we keep doing that, someday we can return to live with Heavenly and Jesus forever. Jesus died for all the world, but He also died for you and me.

Resources

(Select one from each category.)

Children's Songbook
- Tell Me the Stories of Jesus (57)
- I Feel My Savior's Love (74)

Hymn
- I Know That My Redeemer Lives (136)
- I Stand All Amazed (193)

Gospel Art Book
- Jesus Praying in Gethsemane (56)
- The Crucifixion (57)

Scriptures
- Job 19:25
- D&C 49:5

He knows and loves us each individually. Because of this, you can say that Jesus is your personal Savior and Redeemer.

Read and discuss D&C 93:8–9.

+ What is "the Word"?
+ Why is Jesus called "the light and the Redeemer of the world"?
+ What does this phrase mean: "in him was the life of men and the light of men"?

Activity

Younger Children: Look through the *Friend* magazine for pictures of Jesus. Cut them out and glue them on a piece of paper to make a poster. Hang the finished poster in your room so you can remember to follow Jesus Christ.
Older Children: See page 18.

Challenge

Bearing your testimony is a great way to make it stronger. Next fast Sunday, bear your testimony of the Savior during fast and testimony meeting. If this is too hard, you may bear your testimony during FHE.

Challenge

I commit to bear my testimony:
❑   in fast and testimony meeting
❑   next week during family home evening

_____
Signature

_____
Date

Hidden Message

On the following page, color each square with a heart in it. Then write each letter, in order, on the spaces below to reveal what the prophet Job said in Job 19:25. *Solution on page 136.*

___ ___ ___ ___ ___ ___

___ ___ ___ ___ ___ ___ ___

___ ___ ___ ___ ___ ___ ___ ___ ___

___ ___ ___ ___ ___ ___ ___'

___ ___ ___ ___ ___ ___ ___

___ ___ ___ ___ ___ ___ ___

___ ___ ___ ___ ___ ___ ___ ___

___ ___ ___ ___ ___ ___ ___ ___ ___ ___

___ ___ ___

___ ___ ___ ___ ___ ___

___ ___ ___ ___ ___ .

♡	I	♡	♡	K	♡	N	♡	O	♡	W
T	H	♡	A	T	♡	M	♡	♡	Y	♡
R	♡	E	D	♡	E	♡	E	M	♡	E
R	♡	L	♡	♡	I	V	♡	E	♡	T
H	♡	A	N	♡	D	♡	T	♡	H	♡
A	♡	♡	♡	T	♡	H	♡	E	♡	S
H	♡	A	♡	L	♡	L	♡	S	T	♡
♡	♡	A	♡	N	♡	D	♡	A	♡	T
♡	♡	♡	T	♡	H	E	♡	L	♡	A
T	♡	T	E	R	♡	D	♡	A	♡	Y
♡	U	♡	P	♡	O	♡	N	♡	T	H
♡	E	E	♡	A	♡	R	T	♡	H	♡

Through the Atonement of Jesus Christ, all mankind may be saved.

Resources

(Select one from each category.)

Children's Songbook
+ He Sent His Son (34)
+ He Died That We Might Live Again (65)

Hymn
+ I Know That My Redeemer Lives (136)
+ Jesus, Once of Humble Birth (196)

Gospel Art Book
+ Jesus Praying in Gethsemane (56)
+ The Crucifixion (57)

Scriptures
+ John 3:16
+ 1 John 1:7
+ Helaman 5:9

Lesson

Jesus Christ did not die only for the people who hear about His gospel while they live on earth. He died for *everyone*. Many people will die without having the chance to learn about Jesus Christ and His gospel. But that does not mean they are doomed.

Through the Atonement of Jesus Christ, all mankind may be saved. When Jesus's body was in the tomb for three days, His spirit was in the spirit world, organizing missionary work. Those who died without a knowledge of Jesus Christ were then taught by those who had accepted the gospel in this life. We can do temple work for the people who have died without the gospel, and they can choose in the spirit world if they will accept it.

Heavenly Father and Jesus Christ love us deeply. They do not want to lose even one soul because each soul is precious. Through the Atonement of Jesus Christ, all people who ever lived or will live on the earth will have a chance to accept Jesus Christ as their Savior.

Read and discuss Mosiah 3:19–20.

+ What is the natural man? How do we get rid of the natural man within us?
+ What are some of the qualities we need to develop to be more like Jesus Christ?

Activity

All Ages: Fill a box with heavy objects such as books. (Make sure the box is too heavy for one child to carry it by himself.) Ask a child to carry it across the room. When he tries and discovers that it's too heavy, have another child or a parent help. If it is still too heavy, have a parent carry the box for him. Then read Matthew 11:29. Discuss how Jesus Christ carries our burdens.

Challenge

Jesus Christ carries our burdens. Find a way to help someone you know bear their burdens. If someone is sad, listen to them talk about their problems. If someone is working on a hard task, lend them a hand.

Challenge

This week, I will find a way to help someone bear their burdens.

_____

Signature

_____

Date

Resources

(Select one from each category.)

Children's Songbook

+ Did Jesus Really Live Again? (64)
+ The Lord Gave Me a Temple (153)

Hymn

+ My Redeemer Lives (135)
+ That Easter Morn (198)
+ He Is Risen (199)

Gospel Art Book

+ Burial of Jesus (58)
+ Mary and the Resurrected Jesus Christ (59)

Scriptures

+ Mormon 7:5
+ Alma 40:23

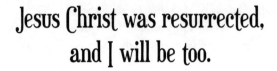

Jesus Christ was resurrected, and I will be too.

Lesson

When Jesus Christ died on the cross for us, His body was placed in a tomb. On the third day, when His disciples went to check on Him, they found His tomb empty. Jesus had overcome death and had been resurrected. His spirit and His body were reunited.

Through the Atonement of Jesus Christ, we too will be resurrected. Our spirits and our bodies will come together again and will be perfected. We will no longer suffer illness or injury. For example, a blind man will be able to see again. A deaf man will hear again. Someone who lost a leg in this life will be able to walk and run perfectly. Resurrection is a gift to everyone on this earth because Heavenly Father and Jesus love us so much.

Read and discuss Mosiah 16:6–9.

+ How is death "swallowed up in Christ"?
+ Why does "the grave hath no victory"?
+ In verse 9, we read that "there can be no more death." Does this mean that since Christ was resurrected no one can die anymore?

Activity

All Ages: Even though we will be resurrected someday, we still need to take care of our bodies. Do a physical activity together as a family. You could go for a walk, go on a bike ride, play a game of soccer, or whatever your family chooses. Afterward, enjoy a nutritious snack.

Challenge

Jesus Christ's Resurrection is an important part of the gospel. This week, find a scripture about the Resurrection not discussed in this lesson. Share it with your family next week during family home evening. An older sibling or parent may help you.

Challenge

I will share the following scripture about the Resurrection with my family next week:

_____

March

God Speaks through Prophets

Prophets are called by God.

Lesson

The prophet is God's representative. He tells us what God would tell us if He were here on earth. Prophets must be called of God. Our prophet today is Thomas Spencer Monson. He holds all the priesthood keys. His two counselors and the Quorum of the Twelve Apostles are also sustained as prophets, but President Monson is the only one with the authority to use all the priesthood keys and is the only one who can receive revelation for the whole Church. He is also the President of The Church of Jesus Christ of Latter-day Saints.

God has called prophets since the beginning of time. Let's read about Moses in the Old Testament.

Read (or summarize) and discuss Moses 1.

+ How did God call Moses to be a prophet?
+ What was Moses to do as a prophet?

Resources

(Select one from each category.)

Children's Songbook
+ Nephi's Courage (120)
+ Latter-day Prophets (134)

Hymn
+ We Thank Thee, O God, for a Prophet (19)
+ God Bless Our Prophet Dear (24)

Gospel Art Book
+ Moses and the Burning Bush (13)
+ Thomas S. Monson (137)

Scriptures
+ Articles of Faith 1:6
+ Numbers 12:6

Activity

Younger Children: Color the picture "Moses Becomes a Prophet" (found in the May 2010 *Friend* magazine; available on lds.org).
Older Children: See page 28.

Challenge

Younger Children: Memorize the names of the First Presidency (Thomas S. Monson, Henry B. Eyring, and Dieter F. Uchtdorf).

Older Children: Memorize the names of the members of the First Presidency and the Quorum of the Twelve Apostles. (First Presidency: Thomas S. Monson, Henry B. Eyring, Dieter F. Uchtdorf. Twelve Apostles: Boyd K. Packer, L. Tom Perry, Russell M. Nelson, Dallin H. Oaks, M. Russell Ballard, Richard G. Scott, Robert D. Hales, Jeffrey R. Holland, David A. Bednar, Quentin L. Cook, D. Todd Christofferson, and Neil L. Andersen.)

Challenge

This week, I will memorize:

❑ The names of the members of the First Presidency

❑ The names of the members of the First Presidency and the Quorum of the Twelve Apostles

Latter-day Prophets

Can you name all of the members of the First Presidency and Quorum of the Twelve Apostles? Write the number under each picture next to the name of the prophet or apostle. **Solution on page 136.**

Photos courtesy of lds.org

1   **2**   **3**

_____ DALLIN H. OAKS

_____ DIETER F. UCHTDORF

_____ M. RUSSELL BALLARD

_____ JEFFREY R. HOLLAND

_____ QUENTIN L. COOK

_____ ROBERT D. HALES

_____ HENRY B. EYRING

_____ L. TOM PERRY

_____ D. TODD CHRISTOFFERSON

_____ BOYD K. PACKER

_____ RICHARD G. SCOTT

_____ NEIL L. ANDERSEN

_____ RUSSELL M. NELSON

_____ THOMAS S. MONSON

_____ DAVID A. BEDNAR

4   5   6   7

8   9   10   11

12   13   14   15

Resources

(Select one from each category.)

Children's Songbook
+ Samuel Tells of the Baby Jesus (36)
+ Latter-day Prophets (134)

Hymn
+ We Listen to a Prophet's Voice (22)
+ The Iron Rod (274)

Gospel Art Book
+ Isaiah Writes of Christ's Birth (22)
+ Abinadi before King Noah (75)

Scriptures
+ Acts 10:42–43
+ D&C 20:21–26

Prophets testify of Jesus Christ.

Lesson

Since the beginning of time, the prophets have testified of Jesus Christ. Before Jesus was born, they prophesied that He would come to earth and be our Savior and Redeemer. After the Savior's birth, the prophets taught that Jesus came to earth and died for our sins. The prophets frequently testify of Jesus Christ because they want us to gain our own testimonies of the Savior and repent of our sins. Following the Savior is the only way we can return to our Heavenly Father.

Abinadi was a prophet in the Book of Mormon who taught the wicked King Noah about Jesus Christ. Though King Noah refused to follow Abinadi's counsel, Abinadi never denied his testimony, even when he was killed. Abinadi taught King Noah that all prophets testify of Jesus Christ.

Read and discuss Mosiah 13:3–5.

+ Why have all the prophets testified of Jesus Christ?
+ How can you gain your own testimony of the Savior?

Activity

All Ages: Go to the Church's website and watch videos of the prophet and apostles bearing witness of Jesus Christ. A video collection entitled *Special Witnesses of Christ* can be found at https://www.lds.org/prophets-and-apostles/what-are-prophets-testimonies?lang=eng.

Challenge

Find an opportunity this week to bear your testimony of Jesus Christ. It doesn't have to be during a formal occasion such as fast and testimony meeting. You can write it in your journal, share it with a family member, or even bear it through your actions (like being a good example or standing up for what you know is right).

Challenge

This week, I commit to bear my testimony of Jesus Christ to a family member or friend, or through my actions.

_____

Signature

_____

Date

There is safety in following the prophet.

Lesson

Lehi was a prophet in Jerusalem in 600 BC. God commanded him to take his family into the wilderness. The people in Jerusalem were wicked, and the city was about to be destroyed because they would not repent.

Lehi and his family left their home and riches behind. It was difficult for them to leave, and they experienced many trials on their way to the promised land. But after they arrived, Lehi had a vision and saw that Jerusalem had been destroyed. If his family had remained there, they would have perished also. Lehi's family was blessed for following the prophet. Let's read in the Book of Mormon about those blessings.

Read and discuss 2 Nephi 1:4–5.

+ What were some of the blessings Lehi's family received for leaving Jerusalem?
+ What are some of the blessings you have received for following the prophet?

Activity

Younger Children: See page 34.

Older Children: Following the prophet makes us happy. Print the smiley face on page 35 from the resource CD. Cut out the smile at the bottom of the page and hang the yellow smiley face on the wall. Play "Pin the Smile on the Happy Face." Blindfold each player when it is his turn and give him directions so he can put the smile on the happy face. Afterward, discuss how listening to the prophet's directions helps us to be happy.

Challenge

With your family, review conference talks or a message from the First Presidency in the *Ensign*. Find one principle the prophet teaches that your family can work on this week. For example, if you read an article about food storage, pick one item you can buy this week to add to your food storage. (You don't have to spend a lot of money. Purchasing even one can of vegetables or soup will help.)

Challenge

This week with my family, I will work on the following principle:

_____

_____

Signature

_____

Date

Follow the Prophet

This boy made some poor choices and is separated from his family. If he follows the prophet, he can return to them. Help him follow each **P** (for prophet) so he can be with his family. *Solution on page 136.*

Resources

(Select one from each category.)

Children's Songbook
- Seek the Lord Early (108)
- The Seventh Article of Faith (126b)

Hymn
- The Voice of God Again Is Heard (18)
- Hark, All Ye Nations! (264)

Gospel Art Book
- The Ten Commandments (14)

Scriptures
- D&C 43:1–7
- 1 Nephi 22:1–2

God speaks through prophets.

Lesson

Heavenly Father is not here on the earth with us, but He still wants to communicate with us and guide us. That's why He speaks through prophets. A prophet is often called the Lord's mouthpiece because he tells us the mind and will of the Lord. He tells us what God would tell us if He were here.

Moses told Pharaoh to free the children of Israel. Lehi commanded the people of Jerusalem to repent. In our day, the prophets have told us to repent of our sins, hold family home evening, and obtain food storage. Whenever the prophet speaks, we should treat his words as God's own words.

Read and discuss D&C 1:38.

- Why does God speak through prophets?
- How should we treat the prophets' words?

Activity

All Ages: Each picture on page 38 represents something about President Thomas S. Monson. Print the pictures from the resource CD. On the back of each picture, write a fact about President Monson. (For example, on the picture of the pigeon, write: "As a boy, he raised prize-winning pigeons." See the list below for the remaining facts.) Put the pictures in a paper bag or a box. Take turns choosing a picture from the bag and reading about President Monson.

Facts about President Monson*

1. He was born in Salt Lake City, Utah.
2. As a boy, he raised prize-winning pigeons.
3. He married Frances Beverly Johnson in the Salt Lake Temple.
4. He served as a mission president in Canada.
5. He became a bishop at age 22.
6. He worked for the *Deseret News*.
7. He was called to be an Apostle at age 36.

* http://www.lds.org/prophets-and-apostles/what-are-prophets/bio/thomas-s-monson?lang=eng

Challenge

The first weekend of April, watch or listen to all four sessions of general conference. Write down at least three things the prophet or apostles tell us we should do.

Challenge

I commit to watch or listen to general conference with my family and write down three things the prophet tells us we should do.

_____

Signature

_____

Date

April

Jesus Christ Restored the
Fulness of the Gospel through
Joseph Smith

Heavenly Father and Jesus Christ appeared to Joseph Smith.

Lesson

When Joseph Smith was fourteen years old, he was very confused about which church to join. After reading James 1:5 in the Bible, he knew he could pray and ask Heavenly Father for help. Joseph went into a grove of trees near his home in upstate New York and asked Heavenly Father which church he should join. He received an unexpected answer. Heavenly Father and Jesus Christ appeared to Joseph and told him to join none of the churches. They explained to him that Christ's true Church was not on the earth. Joseph was called to be the first prophet of the latter days. He had many sacred responsibilities to restore the true Church of Christ and translate the Book of Mormon.

Read and discuss JS—H 1:15–20.

+ Why did Joseph Smith pray in the grove of trees?
+ How was Joseph's prayer answered?
+ How have your own prayers been answered?

Resources

(Select one from each category.)

Children's Songbook

+ This Is My Beloved Son (76)
+ The Sacred Grove (87)
+ On a Golden Springtime (88)

Hymn

+ Joseph Smith's First Prayer (26)
+ Praise to the Man (27)

Gospel Art Book

+ Joseph Smith Seeks Wisdom in the Bible (89)
+ The First Vision (90)

Scriptures

+ James 1:5
+ D&C 1:17

Activity

All Ages: Watch the video "The Restoration," available at https://www.lds.org/media-library/video/2008-06-01-the-restoration?lang=eng.

Challenge

Invite a friend or neighbor over for family home evening. Share Joseph Smith's story with them and invite them to take the missionary discussions. You can invite them next time you see them, over the phone, or through a formal invitation that you create yourself.

Challenge

I will invite _____ over for family

home evening on this day: _____.

_____

Signature

_____

Date

Joseph Smith translated the Book of Mormon by the power of God.

Lesson

Three years after the First Vision, the angel Moroni appeared to Joseph Smith and told him God had a special work for him to do. Joseph was to translate the gold plates, a record of the people in ancient America. Jesus had visited these people and established His Church among them, just as He did with the people in the Bible.

After several more years of preparation, Joseph received the gold plates at the Hill Cumorah. Joseph did not know the language the gold plates were written in, but that did not matter. Joseph also received the Urim and Thummim, which helped him to translate the sacred record. With the help of God, Joseph was able to complete the translation.

Read and discuss JS—H 1:59–60.

+ What did Joseph Smith receive in addition to the gold plates?
+ Why did so many people want the gold plates? How did Joseph keep them safe?
+ Do you know where the gold plates are today?

Resources

(Select one from each category.)

Children's Songbook
+ An Angel Came to Joseph Smith (86a)
+ Book of Mormon Stories (118)

Hymn
+ Truth Eternal (4)
+ An Angel from on High (13)

Gospel Art Book
+ Moroni Appears to Joseph Smith in His Room (91)
+ Joseph Smith Translating the Book of Mormon (92)

Scriptures
+ 2 Nephi 3:11
+ Isaiah 11:1

Activity

Younger Children: See page 44.
Older Children: See page 45.

Challenge

Read from the Book of Mormon with your family each day this week. It's okay if you can only spend a few minutes doing this, but be sure to discuss what you have read and ask your parents any questions you may have.

Challenge

Each day this week, I will read from the Book of Mormon with my family.

_____
Signature

_____
Date

Secret Code

Using the key below, decode the message at the bottom of the page. This activity will give you an idea of what Joseph Smith went through when he translated the Book of Mormon. **Solution on page 136.**

A = 1	H = 8	O = 1 5	V = 2 2
B = 2	I = 9	P = 1 6	W = 2 3
C = 3	J = 1 0	Q = 1 7	X = 2 4
D = 4	K = 1 1	R = 1 8	Y = 2 5
E = 5	L = 1 2	S = 1 9	Z = 2 6
F = 6	M = 1 3	T = 2 0	
G = 7	N = 1 4	U = 2 1	

$$\overline{20} \quad \overline{8} \quad \overline{5}$$

$$\overline{2} \quad \overline{15} \quad \overline{15} \quad \overline{11}$$

$$\overline{15} \quad \overline{6}$$

$$\overline{13} \quad \overline{15} \quad \overline{18} \quad \overline{13} \quad \overline{15} \quad \overline{14}$$

Secret Code

Using the key below, decode the message at the bottom of the page. This activity will give you an idea of what Joseph Smith went through when he translated the Book of Mormon. ***Solution on page 136.***

A = ☆	G = ✪	M = ⇨	S = ♥	Y = ◉
B = ⬤	H = ★	N = ◁	T = ▶	Z = ☆
C = ☆	I = ◉	O = ➜	U = ◀	
D = □	J = ☆	P = ◀	V = ★	
E = ★	K = ☆	Q = ♡	W = ♥	
F = ★	L = ★	R = ▣	X = O	

April, Week Two • 45

Jesus Christ restored the gospel through Joseph Smith.

Lesson

After Joseph Smith translated the Book of Mormon, he was given another great responsibility: to restore the true Church that Christ had established when He was on the earth. On May 15, 1829, John the Baptist came to Joseph Smith and Oliver Cowdery and restored the Aaronic Priesthood. Joseph and Oliver then baptized each other. They later received the Melchizedek priesthood. On April 6, 1830, the Church was officially restored when they held the first meeting.

The Church of Jesus Christ of Latter-day Saints is organized the same way the Church of Christ was in ancient times. Under the direction of Jesus Christ, the Church is led by prophets, apostles, and other priesthood leaders (see Articles of Faith 1:6). The prophet has the authority to receive revelation from God and Jesus Christ, and we can each receive personal revelation.

Read and discuss Ephesians 2:19–20.

+ What is a fellow citizen of the Saints?
+ Who comprises the foundation of the Church?

Resources

(Select one from each category.)

Children's Songbook
+ I Belong to The Church of Jesus Christ of Latter-day Saints (77)
+ The Priesthood Is Restored (89)

Hymn
+ The Morning Breaks (1)
+ High on the Mountain Top (5)

Gospel Art Book
+ John the Baptist Conferring the Aaronic Priesthood (93)
+ Melchizedek Priesthood Restoration (94)

Scriptures
+ Daniel 2:45
+ D&C 110:16

Activity

All Ages: Build a tower with blocks. Explain that each block represents an apostle. Remove the blocks, one by one, until the tower falls. Explain that the Church of Christ cannot stand without its foundation. Rebuild the tower and explain how Joseph Smith restored the Church.

Challenge

Talk to someone who has the priesthood and ask him what blessings he has received by holding the priesthood. Then talk to someone who does not hold the priesthood. Ask him or her how the priesthood has blessed his or her life.

Challenge

This week, I will talk to _____

and _____ about the blessings of

the priesthood.

_____

Signature

_____

Date

May

Principles and Ordinances of the
Gospel Lead Me to Jesus Christ

Resources

(Select one from each category.)

Children's Songbook
+ I Pray in Faith (14)
+ Faith (96)
+ Choose the Right Way (160)

Hymn
+ Lead, Kindly Light (97)
+ Choose the Right (239)

Scriptures
+ James 2:20
+ D&C 20:25, 29
+ 1 Nephi 3:7

My faith in Jesus Christ is strengthened when I obey.

Lesson

The first principle of the gospel is faith in the Lord Jesus Christ. If we do not have faith, then nothing else matters. It is difficult to keep the commandments and repent of our sins if we do not have faith. We cannot be baptized and receive the gift of the Holy Ghost if we do not have faith.

Sometimes it is hard to have faith. But it will grow as we put it to work. The prophet Alma taught that faith is like a seed. If we plant it, it will grow. (See Alma 32.) That means if we keep the commandments, even though it's hard, our faith in Jesus Christ will grow. When we obey, we can better understand why God asks us to do certain things. Our faith will be strengthened so that the next time we are asked to do something, it will be easier to obey. When we have faith, we will witness miracles.

Read and discuss Hebrews 11:1–8, 17–30.

+ What is faith?
+ What miracles have resulted from faith?
+ What can you do to strengthen your faith?

Activity

Younger Children: Color the picture on page 52.
Older Children: See page 53.

Challenge

This week, do something that is difficult for you. Pray and ask Heavenly Father to help you accomplish it, and then exercise your faith in Jesus Christ and do it. This may include bearing your testimony, expressing your emotions (like telling someone you love them), making a new friend, and so forth. Next week during family home evening, share your experience with your family.

Challenge

This week, I will pray for help to do the following:

_____

_____
Signature

_____
Date

Faith is like a little seed: If planted it will grow.
—*Children's Songbook, 96*

Faith Scramble

Unscramble the names of the flowers below. Then write the name of the flower in the corresponding boxes in the grid. When you have finished, the shaded boxes will spell a word that completes the scripture at the bottom of the page. **Solution on page 136.**

1. CHDRIO   4. RESO

2. FODFALID   5. SAIYD

3. ITLUP

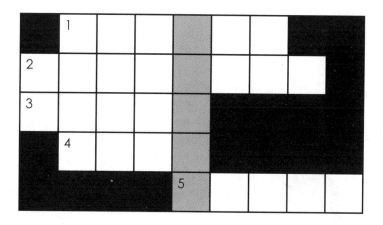

Faith is the substance of things _____ for, the evidence of things not seen (Hebrews 11:1).

Resources

(Select one from each category.)

Children's Songbook
+ Repentance (98)
+ Help Me, Dear Father (99)
+ The Fourth Article of Faith (124)

Hymn
+ Come unto Jesus (117)
+ As Now We Take the Sacrament (169)

Scriptures
+ Isaiah 1:18
+ D&C 58:42
+ 2 Nephi 2:21

I can repent.

Lesson

Through the Atonement, we can repent of our sins. Jesus Christ washes away our sins and makes us clean again, as if the sin never happened.

How do we repent? First, we must admit we have done something wrong and feel sorry that we sinned. Next, we must confess our sins both to God and anyone we have sinned against. Then we must forsake our sins, which means we promise never to commit that sin again. We must also make restitution. That means we should try to make our wrongs right. If we have stolen something, we should return it to the person from whom we stole it. If we hurt someone's feelings, we must sincerely apologize. If we have done all these things with a sincere and honest heart, God will forgive us and remember our sins no more. It is important to repent daily and always keep the commandments as best we can. And we must be willing to forgive others in order for God to forgive us.

Read and discuss Mosiah 4:4–12.

+ What are the steps to repentance?
+ What happens to our sins when we repent?

Activity

Younger Children: Watch and discuss "The Shiny Bicycle" (available at https://www.lds.org/media-library/video/2013-08-011-the-shiny-bicycle?lang=eng).

Older Children: Fill a jar (or another clear container) with water. Add two tablespoons of vinegar. Discuss how the clear water is like our spirits before we sin. Add a couple drops of food coloring to the water. Discuss how the food coloring is like sin and that only a little bit makes a big difference. Next, pour bleach in the jar and watch the water turn clear again. Discuss how repenting cleanses us from sin.

Challenge

Sometimes we sin without even thinking about it. This could include calling someone a name, fighting with your siblings, or being dishonest when your parents ask if you have finished your chores. Every day this week, make an effort to notice your sins as they happen. Repent right away by apologizing to the person you offended, and then praying to Heavenly Father and asking for forgiveness. When we repent right away, we draw closer to Heavenly Father and Jesus Christ and are worthy to have the Holy Ghost with us.

Challenge

This week, I will make an effort to repent immediately after each time I sin, even if it is only a small mistake.

_____
Signature

_____
Date

Week THREE

Resources

(Select one from each category.)

Children's Songbook
+ Baptism (100)
+ When I Am Baptized (103)

Hymn
+ Lead Me into Life Eternal (45)
+ Come, Follow Me (116)
+ Lord, Accept into Thy Kingdom (236)

Gospel Art Book
+ John the Baptist Baptizing Jesus (35)
+ Girl Being Baptized (104)

Scriptures
+ 3 Nephi 27:5
+ D&C 18:21–24
+ Galatians 3:27

When I am baptized, I make a covenant with God.

Lesson

Faith and repentance lead to baptism. When we are baptized, we start a new life as a child of Christ. We become members of The Church of Jesus Christ of Latter-day Saints and enter the gate that leads to the celestial kingdom.

When we are baptized, we make a sacred covenant with God. A covenant is a two-way promise. We make promises to God, and He makes promises to us. Let's read about these covenants in the scriptures.

Read and discuss the baptismal covenant in Mosiah 18:7–17; D&C 20:37; D&C 20:77; and Alma 7:15–16.

+ What do we promise Heavenly Father when we are baptized?
+ What does Heavenly Father promise us?

Activity

Younger Children: See page 62.
Older Children: See page 58.

Challenge

Memorize the covenants we make with Heavenly Father when we are baptized. Look for ways in your daily life to keep those covenants. For example, we promise to serve others when we are baptized. If you see someone at school who needs help, offer to help that person. Even if you haven't been baptized yet, you can practice by always doing what Jesus would do.

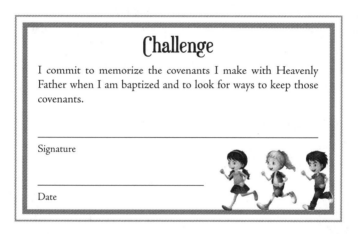

Challenge

I commit to memorize the covenants I make with Heavenly Father when I am baptized and to look for ways to keep those covenants.

_____

Signature

_____

Date

Crossword Puzzle
BAPTISM
Solution on page 136.

ACROSS

2. When we are baptized, we promise to always _____ Jesus.
5. The second principle of the gospel.
9. Jesus taught that we must be baptized by _____ (go all the way under the water).
10. The first principle of the gospel.

DOWN

1. Before getting baptized, we must have a _____ and believe that the Church is true.
3. When we are baptized, we covenant to obey all of the _____.
4. When we are baptized, we make a _____ with God.
6. How old must a person be to get baptized?
7. When we get baptized, we become a member of The _____ of Jesus Christ of Latter-day Saints.
8. If we keep our baptismal covenant, Heavenly Father will give us eternal _____.

Resources

(Select one from each category.)

Children's Songbook
* I Know My Father Lives (5)
* The Holy Ghost (105)
* The Still Smal Voice (106)

Hymn
* The Spirit of God (2)
* Dearest Children, God Is Near You (96)

Gospel Art Book
* The Gift of the Holy Ghost (105)

Scriptures
* Matthew 3:11
* Acts 2:38

When I am confirmed, I receive the gift of the Holy Ghost.

Lesson

Before we are baptized, the Holy Ghost can come to us at certain times, but He does not stay with us. After we are baptized, we are confirmed members of The Church of Jesus Christ of Latter-day Saints and receive the gift of the Holy Ghost. This ordinance is often called the baptism of fire because the Holy Ghost sanctifies and purifies us.

When we receive the gift of the Holy Ghost, the Holy Ghost becomes our constant companion. He will not leave us as long as we are worthy and keep the commandments.

Having the constant companionship of the Holy Ghost is one of God's greatest gifts to us. The Holy Ghost can guide us and warn us of danger. He can comfort us when we are sad. He can help us remember things and help us understand gospel principles. We can always rely on the Holy Ghost to help us make the right choices.

Read and discuss 2 Nephi 31:17 and D&C 84:64.

* Who will receive the gift of the Holy Ghost?

- Why is receiving the Holy Ghost called the baptism by fire?
- What do we need to do to keep this gift?

Activity

All Ages: Parents, before family home evening, look up a few scriptures in the Topical Guide about the Holy Ghost. Write the scripture reference on a small piece of paper. Wrap each scripture in a small box. Let your children take turns opening each gift and looking up the scripture. Discuss how the gift of the Holy Ghost is one of God's greatest gifts to us.

Challenge

Before making any decisions this week, stop and ask yourself if your decision will allow you to be worthy of the Holy Ghost.

Challenge

Before making any decisions this week, I will stop and ask myself if my decision will allow me to be worthy of the Holy Ghost.

_____
Signature

_____
Date

Color each square with an 8 in it. Then write each letter, in order, on the spaces below to reveal an important word about baptism. *Solution on page 136.*

8	C	8	8	8	8	8
8	8	O	8	8	8	8
8	8	8	8	8	V	8
E	8	8	8	N	8	8
8	8	8	A	8	8	N
8	8	T	8	8	8	8

___ ___ ___ ___ ___ ___ ___ ___

June

The Holy Ghost Testifies of the Truth of All Things

The Holy Ghost is the third member of the Godhead.

Lesson

There are three members of the Godhead: Heavenly Father, Jesus Christ, and the Holy Ghost. They all work together to help us come unto Christ and return to our Heavenly Father. Though Heavenly Father and Jesus Christ have bodies of flesh and bone, the Holy Ghost is a personage of spirit (see D&C 130:22). Because He is a spirit, His influence can be felt everywhere. Some people compare the influence of the Holy Ghost to the sun. Everyone can feel the sun's warmth and see its light.

The Holy Ghost plays several roles in the plan of salvation: testifying of truth, revealing the word of God, guiding and warning us, sanctifying us when we are baptized, and comforting us. The Holy Ghost has several different names: the Spirit, the Holy Spirit, the Spirit of the Lord, the Spirit of God, and the Comforter.

We are separated from Heavenly Father and Jesus while we are here on earth. Fortunately, the Holy Ghost can be our constant companion and help us to feel close to them anytime, anywhere.

Resources

(Select one from each category.)

Children's Songbook
+ The Holy Ghost (105)
+ The First Article of Faith (122a)

Hymn
+ The Spirit of God (2)
+ The Light Divine (305)

Scriptures
+ Romans 14:17
+ D&C 84:88
+ 1 Corinthians 2:11

Read and discuss D&C 130:22.

+ Why is the Holy Ghost a spirit?
+ How can the Holy Ghost dwell in us?

Activity

Younger Children: See page 66.
Older Children: See page 67.

Challenge

Though they are three separate beings, the members of the Godhead are one in purpose. This week, learn what it's like to be unified with your family and work together. Complete a project that all of you can help with. Not everyone will be able to contribute equally. Young children will not be able to perform the same tasks as older children or adults. But everyone should have a job according to his or her age and skill level.

Next week during family home evening, discuss how you felt while working together.

Challenge

This week, our family will work together on the following project:

_____

_____

_____

The Comforter

Some people compare the Holy Ghost to a blanket (or comforter) because one of the names of the Holy Ghost is the Comforter. The Holy Ghost makes us feel warm inside and helps us feel safe. In each square of the blanket below, write down a way the Holy Ghost can help us.

Missing Vowels

THE HOLY GHOST

Below is a scripture from Doctrine and Covenants. Fill in all the missing vowels to discover what it says about the Holy Ghost. *Solution on page 136.*

```
A A A A A A A A A A A A A A A   E E E E E E E E E E E E E E
I I I I I   O O O O O O O O O O O O O O O O O O O O   U U U U
```

TH___ F__TH__R H__S ___ B__DY __F

FL__SH __ND B__N__S __S T__NG__BL__

__S M__N'S; TH___ S__N __LS__; B__T

TH___ H__LY GH__ST H__S N__T ___

B__DY __F FL__SH __ND B__N__S, B__T

__S __ P__RS__N__G__ __F SP__R__T.

W__R__ __T N__T S__, TH___ H__LY

GH__ST C__ __LD N__T DW__LL IN ___S.

—D&C 130:22

Week TWO

Resources

(Select one from each category.)

Children's Songbook
+ The Still Small Voice (106)
+ Listen, Listen (107)

Hymn
+ Let the Holy Spirit Guide (143)
+ I Know My Father Lives (302)

Scriptures
+ D&C 6:23
+ D&C 85:6
+ D&C 8:2
+ John 14:26

The Holy Ghost speaks in a still, small voice.

Lesson

We are told that the Holy Ghost speaks in a still, small voice. What does that mean? Does He whisper to us? Does He speak so quietly we can barely hear Him? Some people do hear a gentle voice, but many people say they do not actually hear a voice when the Holy Ghost speaks to them. Rather, they have a peaceful feeling. Some people have a warm feeling come over them. Some have a strong feeling they should do something, and others have thoughts that they know are not their own.

We must live in such a way that we will always hear and feel the promptings of the Holy Ghost. If we are too busy to focus on spiritual things, we will probably miss the promptings from the Spirit.

Read and discuss the fruits of the Spirit in Galatians 5:22–23.

+ What are some of the ways the Holy Ghost manifests Himself unto us?
+ Can you think of a time when the Holy Ghost prompted you to do something?

Activity

Younger Children: Color the picture on page 70.
Older Children: See page 71.

Challenge

This week, practice listening to the still, small voice. After you say your personal prayers at night, sit quietly for a few minutes and listen to the promptings of the Holy Ghost.

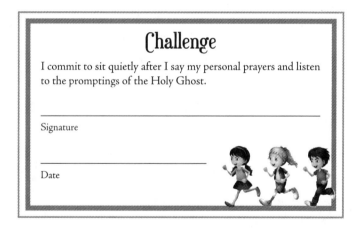

Challenge

I commit to sit quietly after I say my personal prayers and listen to the promptings of the Holy Ghost.

_____

Signature

_____

Date

The **fruit of the Spirit** is love, joy, peace, longsuffering, gentleness, goodness, faith, meekness, temperance: against such there is no law (Galatians 5:22–23).

The Fruit of the Spirit

Unscramble the words below to name some of the fruit of the Spirit that Paul mentioned in Galatians 5:22–23. *Solution on page 136.*

Fruit

1. VOLE
2. OJY
3. APEEC
4. SENETELGNS
5. OONESGDS
6. IATFH

1. _____

2. _____

3. _____

4. _____

5. _____

6. _____

Resources

(Select one from each category.)

Children's Songbook
+ The Still Small Voice (106)
+ Listen, Listen (107)

Hymn
+ Let the Holy Spirit Guide (143)
+ Thy Spirit, Lord, Has Stirred Our Souls (157)

Scriptures
+ D&C 11:12
+ Romans 8:27
+ 1 John 4:6
+ 2 Nephi 32:5

The Holy Ghost can guide and protect us.

Lesson

Nephi and his brothers faced many challenges when they tried to obtain the brass plates from Laban. First, Laban stole the valuable items the brothers offered Laban for the plates. Then Laban tried to kill them. Laman and Lemuel were angry, but Nephi knew they could not give up.

Nephi went to Laban's house again, having faith that he would be guided and protected. He said, "And I was led by the Spirit, not knowing beforehand the things which I should do." Nephi was in a very scary situation, but he knew the Holy Ghost would be there to guide him. Let's read about Nephi's experience in the Book of Mormon.

Read (or summarize) and discuss 1 Nephi 4:6–38.

+ How did the Holy Ghost help Nephi?
+ How has the Holy Ghost guided and protected you?

Activity

All Ages: Play sounds your children are familiar with that signify an event: the phone ringing, the doorbell, the car starting, a timer, someone knocking at the door, an alarm clock ringing, and so forth. Explain that these signs all represent something that is taking place. For example, when the phone rings, we know someone wants to talk to us. When an alarm clock rings, it is time to get up. Liken this to the promptings of the Holy Ghost. When we feel peace, the Holy Ghost is telling us to go ahead and do something. When we have a stupor of thought or a bad feeling, the Holy Ghost is warning us not to do something.

Challenge

This week, pay attention to how the Holy Ghost speaks to you. For example, when you do something right (like help someone in need or go to church), stop and pay attention to your feelings. Do you feel good inside? Do you feel peace?

Challenge

This week, I will pay attention to how the Holy Ghost speaks to me.

_____

Signature

_____

Date

Resources

(Select one from each category.)

Children's Songbook
+ The Holy Ghost (105)
+ Search, Ponder, and Pray (109)

Hymn
+ Testimony (137)
+ I Know My Father Lives (302)

Scriptures
+ John 15:26
+ 3 Nephi 11:36
+ D&C 9:8
+ 1 Corinthians 12:3

By the power of the Holy Ghost, we may know the truth of all things.

Lesson

It can be difficult to know if what we are taught is true. But God does not want us to remain confused. He has promised to send the Holy Ghost to help us.

When Lehi took his family into the wilderness, Nephi and his brothers wondered if their father really did have a vision that Jerusalem would be destroyed. Even though Nephi was righteous, leaving his home was difficult. But he prayed to know if his father's words were true, and the Holy Ghost comforted him and told him that they were (see 1 Nephi 2:16–17).

We can do the same. Whenever we have doubts about something being true (the scriptures, the words of the prophets, and so forth), we can pray and ask God. He will send the Holy Ghost to tell us what is right.

Read and discuss Moroni 10:3–5.

+ When we want to know the truth, do we simply ask God, or do we need to do something else first?
+ How does the Holy Ghost manifest truth?

Activity

All Ages: Before family home evening begins, write a message to your children with invisible ink. Dip a Q-tip or paintbrush in some milk and write a message on a piece of paper. During family home evening, give your children the message written in invisible ink. Turn the stove on low, and help them hold it about twelve inches above the burner, until the message appears. (If the message does not appear, you may need to turn up the heat; however, be careful not to light the paper on fire.) Explain to your children that the heat from the stove is like the Holy Ghost. He helps us to see things that are not obvious and tells us the truth of all things.

Challenge

Before you go to Primary next Sunday, say a special prayer and ask Heavenly Father to help you know that the things you will be learning are true. Pay attention to how you feel during Primary. Do you feel peace? Do you have a warm feeling inside? This is the Holy Ghost telling you that the gospel is true.

Challenge

Before I go to Primary next Sunday, I will say a special prayer and ask Heavenly Father to help me know that the things I will be learning are true.

_____

Signature

_____

Date

July

I Can Follow
Jesus Christ's Example

Jesus Christ always obeyed Heavenly Father.

Lesson

Jesus Christ is the only perfect person to ever live. He has obeyed Heavenly Father from the beginning, even when it was extremely difficult. When Jesus Christ was on the earth, He was always kind to others. He obeyed all the commandments and was baptized. He always resisted temptation. Most important, He died for our sins. No one can understand how much pain He suffered for us. But He did it because He loves both Heavenly Father and us. When Jesus visited the Nephites in America, He told them who He was and how He had obeyed His Father.

Read and discuss 3 Nephi 11:11.

+ What did Jesus mean when he said he drank out of the bitter cup?
+ How did Christ suffer the will of the Father in all things?

Resources

(Select one from each category.)

Children's Songbook
+ Jesus Once Was a Little Child (55)
+ When Jesus Christ Was Baptized (102)

Hymn
+ Thy Will, O Lord, Be Done (188)
+ Jesus, Once of Humble Birth (196)

Gospel Art Book
+ Jesus Praying with His Mother (33)
+ Boy Jesus in the Temple (34)

Scriptures
+ Matthew 26:39
+ John 8:29

Activity

All Ages: Ask your children to do something that you know they can't do by themselves (lift a heavy object, read something, and so on). If they question your request, express how much you would like them to try. Then help them accomplish the task. Explain that we don't always understand what Heavenly Father asks us to do, and sometimes we can't do it on our own. Reassure them that if they are trying to be obedient, Heavenly Father will help them and give them the strength they need.

Challenge

Obeying our parents helps us learn to obey greater commandments from Heavenly Father. Choose one of your parents' rules that you have trouble with and be completely obedient to it for one week.

Challenge

This week, I will be completely obedient to the following rule:

_____

_____

Signature

_____

Date

Resources

(Select one from each category.)

Children's Songbook
* Tell Me the Stories of Jesus (57)
* Jesus Loved the Little Children (59)

Hymn
* Abide with Me (166)
* How Great the Wisdom and the Love (195)

Gospel Art Book
* Christ Healing the Sick at Bethesda (42)
* Jesus Carrying a Lost Lamb (64)

Scriptures
* 1 Nephi 22:25
* Alma 5:57
* Alma 5:38

Jesus Christ went about doing good.

Lesson

Jesus told His disciples, "I am the good shepherd: the good shepherd giveth his life for the sheep" (John 10:11). A shepherd does everything he can to take care of his sheep and make sure they are safe. He gives the sheep food and water and will even risk his life to save them if they are in danger.

Jesus gave His life for all of us—not just when He died on the cross, but also through the service He gave when He was on the earth. Jesus's life was different from everyone else's. He could not do whatever He wanted. He had a very special mission to fulfill from Heavenly Father and spent His life serving others. He taught people the way back to the Father. He healed the sick and raised the dead. He established His Church. And most important, He paid the price for all our sins. Jesus is the perfect example of how to live a good life.

Read and discuss John 10:14–16.

* Why did Jesus call Himself "the good shepherd"?
* How does Jesus know His sheep?

Activity

All Ages: Do a service project together as a family. You could visit an elderly neighbor, do a chore for a neighbor, take someone dinner or a treat, wash someone's car, do yard work for someone, or do anything else that will brighten someone's day.

Challenge

Look for ways to serve others. You don't have to participate in a service project to give service. You can help someone with their homework, play with a younger sibling, set the table, take out the trash when it isn't your turn, and so forth.

Challenge

Each day this week, I will look for opportunities to serve others.

_____

Signature

_____

Date

Resources

(Select one from each category.)

Children's Songbook
+ I'm Trying to Be Like Jesus (78)
+ Love One Another (136)

Hymn
+ The Lord Is My Light (89)
+ More Holiness Give Me (131)

Gospel Art Book
+ Jesus Cleansing the Temple (51)
+ Jesus Washing the Apostles' Feet (55)

Scriptures
+ Matthew 4:19
+ John 13:15
+ 2 Nephi 31:16

Jesus Christ's example teaches me how to live.

Lesson

Jesus Christ is the perfect example of how to live because He lived a perfect life. He always obeyed Heavenly Father. He was kind and showed love to everyone, always putting others' needs before His own. When He visited the Nephites, He told them it was time for Him to leave. But then He noticed how much they still needed Him and decided to stay. He told them, "Behold my bowels are filled with compassion towards you" (3 Nephi 17:6). Then He invited anyone who was sick or afflicted to come to Him for a blessing. It did not matter to Him that He had planned on leaving. He loved these people and wanted to heal them.

If we follow Jesus's example, we will love and serve one another. We will have a greater desire to keep the commandments, and we will grow closer to Heavenly Father and Jesus Christ.

Read and discuss 3 Nephi 27:27.
+ To whom is Jesus speaking? Does this commandment apply to us as well?

Activity

Younger Children: Draw a picture of someone who is a good example to you.
Older Children: Write letter to someone and thank them for being a good example to you.

Challenge

Each day, we face temptation, even if it isn't a big temptation. It's often easy to forget what is right and fight with our siblings or call someone a name on the playground. This week, make more of an effort to choose the right. Each time you are about to do something questionable, stop and ask yourself, "What would Jesus do?"

Challenge

This week, whenever I am tempted to do something wrong, I will stop and ask myself, "What would Jesus do?

_____

Signature

_____

Date

August

Jesus Christ Is the Son of God, and He Is a God of Miracles

Resources

(Select one from each category.)

Children's Songbook
- He Sent His Son (34)
- I Feel My Savior's Love (74)

Hymn
- Redeemer of Israel (6)
- For the Beauty of the Earth (92)

Gospel Art Book
- Jesus Raising Jairus's Daughter (41)
- Mary and the Resurrected Jesus Christ (59)

Scriptures
- 2 Nephi 27:23
- John 3:2
- D&C 35:8

Jesus Christ is a God of miracles.

Lesson

One day when Jesus was teaching a large crowd, it grew late and He told his disciples to give the people something to eat. But there was no food, except five loaves of bread and two fish. He took the food and broke it and blessed it. Somehow there was enough food to feed all five thousand men and their families. There was even food left over!

Jesus performed a great miracle that day by feeding so many people. He also performed other miracles, such as turning water into wine, calming the stormy sea, healing the sick, walking on water, and raising the dead. When people speak of the miracles Jesus performed, they often mention the ones we just talked about. But the greatest miracle of all is the Atonement. Through Christ's Atonement, we are freed from spiritual and physical death. We will be resurrected and can live with Heavenly Father again if we have obeyed the commandments and repented of our sins. That is the greatest miracle of all.

Read and discuss Moroni 7:27–29.

+ Does Jesus continue to perform miracles today?
+ What are some of the miracles you have seen in your life? (*Explain to your family that not all miracles are as "spectacular" as the ones we read about in the scriptures. A miracle can be as simple as having a prayer answered.*)

Activity

All Ages: Watch a video about Jesus on www.lds.org/bible-videos.

Challenge

Miracles happen every day. Some are big and some are small, but God is constantly watching over us. This week talk to an adult member of your family and ask him or her about a miracle he or she has witnessed. Then record in your journal how you felt as this family member shared his or her sacred experience with you.

Challenge

This week, I will ask the following person about a miracle he or she has witnessed:

_____

_____
Signature

_____
Date

Jesus Christ can heal the sick.

Lesson

Jesus Christ has the power to do all things. That includes the healing the sick. Have you ever been ill and prayed (or had a priesthood blessing) and gotten better? That healing came through the power of Jesus Christ.

Jesus can heal something as simple as a skinned knee or something as complex as cancer. He can even heal us emotionally when our feelings are hurt. When Jesus Christ was on the earth, He spent a lot of time healing the sick and blind.

Read and discuss Mark 5:25–34.

+ Why did the woman touch Jesus's garment?
+ Why was this woman healed?
+ Have you witnessed the healing power of Jesus Christ in your own life?

Activity

Younger Children: Make a get-well card for a friend or family member who is sick.

Older Children: See page 90.

Resources

(Select one from each category.)

Children's Songbook
+ Jesus Said Love Everyone (61)
+ Love One Another (136)

Hymn
+ I Need Thee Every Hour (98)
+ Where Can I Turn for Peace? (129)

Gospel Art Book
+ Christ Healing the Sick at Bethesda (42)
+ The Ten Lepers (46)

Scriptures
+ Psalm 147:3
+ Matthew 4:23
+ 1 Nephi 11:31

Challenge

Jesus Christ has the power to heal all sicknesses, but it takes faith on our part. First, we have to ask to be healed, and then we need to have faith that He can heal us (or the person we're praying for). This week, exercise your faith in Jesus Christ and pray that healing will come to someone in your family, someone in your ward or branch, or someone at school. If you are not aware of anyone who may need your prayers, you can always ask the bishop or branch president for a specific name.

Challenge

This week, I will exercise my faith in Jesus Christ by praying daily for the following person:

_____

_____
Signature

_____
Date

Word Search

MARK 5:25–34

Below is the passage from the book of Mark that we read during our lesson. Find the words in bold in the word search on the next page. *Solution on page 136.*

25 And a certain woman, which had an issue of **blood** twelve years,

26 And had suffered many things of many physicians, and had spent all that she had, and was nothing bettered, but rather grew worse,

27 When she had heard of Jesus, came in the press behind, and touched his **garment**.

28 For she said, If I may touch but his clothes, I shall be **whole**.

29 And straightway the fountain of her blood was dried up; and she felt in her body that she was **healed** of that plague.

30 And Jesus, immediately knowing in himself that **virtue** had gone out of him, turned him about in the press, and said, Who touched my clothes?

31 And his disciples said unto him, Thou seest the multitude thronging thee, and sayest thou, Who touched me?

32 And he looked round about to see her that had done this thing.

33 But the woman fearing and trembling, knowing what was done in her, came and fell down before him, and told him all the **truth**.

34 And he said unto her, Daughter, thy **faith** hath made thee whole; go in peace, and be whole of thy **plague**.

```
P  M  A  I  N  Z  T  U  J  D  D  X  P  M  B  M  H
W  D  E  Z  M  A  E  E  O  P  L  A  G  U  E  Y  X
A  H  X  B  T  C  A  B  F  G  O  F  H  L  Q  H  K
T  W  H  M  C  W  D  Z  F  C  V  O  Q  V  O  E  O
L  T  W  Y  F  N  F  O  Q  V  I  R  T  U  E  A  C
X  P  X  F  F  J  P  I  E  Y  N  C  E  T  D  L  M
T  T  W  A  T  P  E  G  V  L  N  U  I  A  H  E  X
H  R  Z  I  H  A  K  C  Z  Q  X  M  H  U  Y  D  E
O  U  H  T  T  O  T  D  T  G  K  U  D  Q  V  L  G
T  T  D  H  O  V  J  B  K  O  Y  K  E  I  O  G  B
T  H  N  T  W  H  R  H  W  O  M  M  W  H  K  T  S
K  D  Y  G  T  P  P  B  F  F  X  M  W  N  N  Y  J
B  U  R  C  H  P  F  D  L  K  M  X  Y  E  H  R  S
Z  T  F  G  F  Y  O  U  H  O  S  N  M  E  S  P  B
V  Y  T  P  T  S  Z  S  G  L  O  R  D  K  G  B  L
G  N  K  S  O  S  K  B  F  R  A  D  O  J  P  Y  R
R  U  A  V  D  H  Q  L  Y  G  F  A  N  R  E  J  W
```

Week THREE

Resources

(Select one from each category.)

Children's Songbook
- Jesus Has Risen (70)
- The Lord Gave Me a Temple (153)

Hymn
- My Redeemer Lives (135)
- He Is Risen! (199)

Gospel Art Book
- Jesus Raising Jairus's Daughter (41)
- Jesus Shows His Wounds (60)

Scriptures
- John 10:18
- 2 Nephi 9:26
- Isaiah 25:8

Jesus Christ has power over death.

Lesson

When Jesus Christ was on the earth, He raised many people from the dead. A man named Jairus had a daughter who became very ill and died. Jesus raised her from the dead. You may also have heard of Lazarus, whom Jesus raised from the dead after four days.

These were great miracles, but an even greater miracle took place. When Jesus was crucified, His body was laid in a tomb. On the third day, He was resurrected. He overcame death, and His spirit and body were reunited. Because Jesus was resurrected, all of us will be resurrected someday.

Read and discuss the story of Lazarus in John 11.

- Why did Jesus ask Martha if she believed Him before He raised Lazarus from the dead (v. 26)?
- Why did Jesus weep with Mary and Martha, even though He knew He would soon raise Lazarus from the dead?

Activity

All Ages: Watch the Bible video "Jesus Is Resurrected," available at http://www.mormonchannel.org/bible-videos?v=1537265083001.

Challenge

Write a letter to someone who has recently lost a loved one, and share your testimony of the resurrection. (If you don't know how to write yet, a parent or older sibling can help you.) It's okay if the person to whom you write the letter lost someone months ago. They are probably still grieving and would appreciate a kind note.

Challenge

This week, I will write a letter to

_____

and bear my testimony of the resurrection.

Week FOUR

Resources

(Select one from each category.)

Children's Songbook
+ Faith (96)
+ I Pray in Faith (14)

Hymn
+ God Moves in a Mysterious Way (285)
+ I Believe in Christ (134)

Gospel Art Book
+ Jesus Calms the Storm (40)
+ Jesus Walking on the Water (43)

Scriptures
+ 2 Nephi 27:23
+ Matthew 21:21
+ Ether 12:12

Miracles come to those who have faith.

Lesson

Before we can witness a miracle, we need to have faith. Moroni taught, "For if there be no faith among the children of men God can do no miracle among them; wherefore, he showed not himself until after their faith" (Ether 12:12).

Read and discuss Mark 10:46–52.

+ What did Jesus say had made the blind man whole?
+ Why must we have faith before we can experience a miracle?

Some people say that miracles don't happen anymore. But that is not true. We can still experience miracles today, if we have faith. The prophet Mormon taught us why it may appear that miracles have ceased.

Read and discuss Mormon 9:19–20.

+ Why don't some people see miracles today?

Activity

All Ages: Think about some of the miracles your family has experienced. Remember, a miracle doesn't have to be a grand event like the feeding of the five thousand. A miracle occurs every time we see the hand of God in our lives. Compile a list of a few of the miracles your family has witnessed. Keep the list somewhere you will see if often, and continue to add to the list as time goes on. You could make a list in a notebook or on small strips of paper that go into a jar. Periodically read your list of miracles together as a family.

Challenge

Sometime this week, read the story of Jesus and Peter walking on water in Matthew 14:22–33. Discuss the following with your family:

Why was Peter able to walk on water at first? Why did he begin to sink? How can we increase our faith in Jesus Christ?

Challenge

This week I will read and discuss Matthew 14:22–33 with my family.

_____

Signature

_____

Date

September

I Obey Jesus Christ
Because I Love Him

Resources

(Select one from each category.)

Children's Songbook
+ Keep the Commandments (146)
+ Dare to Do Right (158)
+ Choose the Right Way (160)

Hymn
+ How Gentle God's Commands (125)
+ Lord, I Would Follow Thee (220)
+ Do What Is Right (237)

Scriptures
+ 1 John 2:3
+ D&C 93:20
+ Mosiah 2:22

I show love to Jesus Christ when I keep the commandments.

Lesson

Jesus told His disciples, "If ye love me, keep my commandments" (John 14:15). Jesus loves us and has paid a very high price for us to return to Heavenly Father someday. All He asks is that we show our love and gratitude to Him by keeping the commandments. That may sound simple, but sometimes we are tempted and keeping the commandments is difficult. But if we remember how much we love Jesus Christ, we will not want to hurt Him. It will then become easier to make the right choices.

Even as a young boy, the Prophet Joseph Smith loved Jesus Christ a lot. After the First Vision, he felt he could be living a more righteous life. One night, he prayed to know how God felt about him and his actions. That's when the angel Moroni appeared to him and told him of his calling to translate the Book of Mormon. Many hard times followed. Joseph was ridiculed, imprisoned, and persecuted. But he never stopped obeying the commandments because of his deep love for Jesus Christ.

Read and discuss John 15:10.

+ How does our love for Jesus Christ grow when we keep the commandments?
+ How does Jesus Christ show His love for us when we keep the commandments?

Activity

All Ages: See page 106.

Challenge

Obey all of your family's rules for one week. When you are tempted to break a rule, remind yourself that obeying rules shows love for your family and Jesus Christ.

Challenge

This week, I commit to follow all of my family's rules. When I'm tempted to break a rule, I will think of Jesus Christ.

_____

Signature

_____

Date

Resources

(Select one from each category.)

Children's Songbook
+ A Child's Prayer (12)
+ I Pray in Faith (14)
+ Love Is Spoken Here (190)

Hymn
+ Did You Think to Pray? (140)
+ Sweet Hour of Prayer (142)
+ Secret Prayer (144)

Gospel Art Book
+ Young Boy Praying (111)
+ Family Prayer (112)

Scriptures
+ 2 Chronicles 7:14
+ Matthew 7:7
+ Alma 37:37

My love for Jesus Christ grows when I pray.

Lesson

How do we grow closer to our family and friends? We talk to them and tell them what is going on in our lives. If they live too far away to see every day, we can talk to them on the phone or Internet and write letters or emails. We cannot see Heavenly Father, but we can still talk to Him every day. The Apostle Paul told the Thessalonians, "Pray without ceasing" (1 Thessalonians 5:17). This does not mean we have to pray constantly, but it does mean we should pray often.

What should we pray for? Anything that is important to us. We can pray for help with a test at school or for a loved one to recover from an illness. We can pray to know if the prophet's words are true or for comfort when we are sad. But we should always remember to give thanks for our many blessings. When we express gratitude, we remember how much our Savior has done for us and how much He loves us. And in turn, we will remember how much we love Him.

Read and discuss D&C 19:38.

+ How often should we pray?
+ What happens when we pray? Why is this better than the treasures of the earth?

Activity

Younger Children: See page 102.

Older Children: Make a telephone with soup cans and string (see page 103). Go in different rooms and take turns talking to each other. Explain to your children that even though we can't see Heavenly Father, we can pray to Him anytime, anywhere.

Challenge

It's easy to remember to pray with our families and before we go to bed. But it isn't always as easy to pray when we get up in the morning or at other times throughout the day. Each day this week, pray at least once besides the times you usually do. If you are at school or another place where you cannot pray out loud, say a prayer in your heart. Our Heavenly Father will still hear you.

Challenge

This week, I commit to say one extra prayer each day.

_____

Signature

_____

Date

My love for Jesus Christ grows when I pray

Our love for Jesus Christ grows when we pray. In the heart below, draw a picture of something we can pray for.

Prayer is like a telephone

Materials

2 identical soup cans
pointed tool*
5-foot length of string
toothpick (optional)

Instructions

1. In the bottom of each can, punch a small hole. The hole should be big enough for the string to go through but small enough that it won't fall out when knotted.
2. Insert the string through the hole in one of the cans. Tie a knot and pull string tight. If the knot is not big enough and the string slips through the hole, tie the string around a piece of toothpick to hold the string in place.
3. Repeat step 2 with the remaining can and the other end of the string.

* To avoid injury, parents should help children punch holes with the pointed tool.

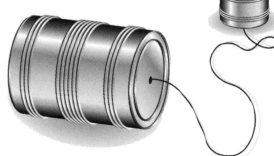

Resources

(Select one from each category.)

Children's Songbook
+ Seek the Lord Early (108)
+ Search, Ponder, and Pray (109)

Hymn
+ The Iron Rod (274)
+ As I Search the Holy Scriptures (277)

Scriptures
+ D&C 11:22
+ 3 Nephi 20:11
+ 3 Nephi 23:14

My love for Jesus Christ grows when I study the scriptures.

Lesson

Each day we feed our bodies with food and water. Without such nourishment, we would die. But it is also very important to feed our spirits every day. How do we do that? By studying the scriptures.

Nephi promised that we would be blessed if we read the scriptures. He said, "Feast upon the words of Christ; for behold, the words of Christ will tell you all things what ye should do" (2 Nephi 32:3). If we study the scriptures, the Holy Ghost will whisper to us the things that we must do. He will fill us with the love of our Savior and help us make good choices. It is impossible to read the scriptures without learning of Jesus Christ and His great sacrifice for us.

Read and discuss John 5:39.
+ What does it mean to search the scriptures?
+ Of whom do the scriptures testify?

Activity

Younger Children: Draw a picture of your favorite scripture story.
Older Children: Have a scripture chase. Pick a topic and have a parent find scriptures in the Topical Guide. The remaining family members see who can look up the scriptures the fastest. You can play individually or divide into teams.

Challenge

Have personal scripture study each day this week. If you can't read on your own yet, look at pictures that depict scripture stories or sing a Primary song like "Book of Mormon Stories."

Challenge

This week, I will have personal scripture study each day.

_____

Signature

_____

Date

I Will Keep the Commandments

Moses received the Ten Commandments on stone tablets like the ones below. Write (or draw) on the tablets some of the commandments you will strive to obey better.

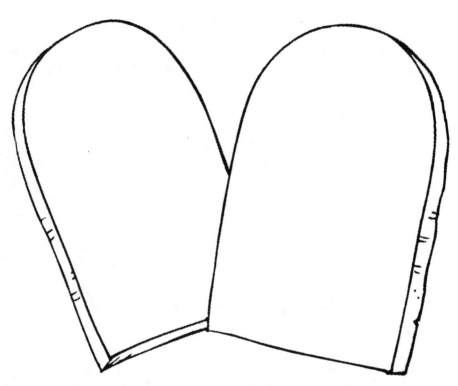

October

The Mission of the Church Is to
Invite All to Come unto Christ

Week ONE

Resources

(Select one from each category.)

Children's Songbook
- Follow the Prophet (110)
- Book of Mormon Stories (118)

Hymn
- Come, Listen to a Prophet's Voice (21)
- Great Is the Lord (77)

Gospel Art Book
- Abinadi before King Noah (75)

Scriptures
- D&C 20:26
- 1 Corinthians 12:28

Following the prophet will help us come unto Christ.

Lesson

In the Book of Mormon we read of Abinadi, a prophet who tried to convince the wicked King Noah to repent. King Noah rejected Abinadi, but Alma, one of his priests, was touched by Abinadi's words. Alma had been taught the gospel before but made many mistakes. After listening to Abinadi, he decided to repent and follow Jesus Christ again.

Alma escaped from King Noah and his servants and hid in the wilderness. He repented of his sins and taught the Nephites the gospel. Many of them were baptized and followed Jesus Christ by serving each other and sharing everything they had.

Imagine what would've happened if Abinadi did not have the courage to teach King Noah, or if Alma did not have the courage to leave King Noah's court. Many people would have been without the gospel. But because Alma had the courage to listen to a prophet of God, many souls were brought unto Christ.

Read and discuss Isaiah 58:1.

+ What is the role of a prophet?
+ Why does the prophet call us to repentance?

Activity

All Ages: Plan a treasure hunt for your children. Hide the treasure, and then place arrows on the wall or on the floor to guide the children to the treasure. The treasure can be anything you want—a treat, a favorite book to read together, materials to make a craft, and so on. Discuss how the children had to follow the arrows in order to find the treasure. Likewise, we need to follow the words of the prophet in order to make it back to Jesus Christ.

Challenge

This past general conference, we listened to many modern-day prophets. Discuss with your family one principle you learned in general conference that you can work on together. Start working on it this week.

Challenge

This week, my family and I will work on the principle of

_____.

_____
Signature

_____
Date

Week TWO

Resources

(Select one from each category.)

Children's Songbook
+ I Want to Be a Missionary Now (168)
+ I Hope They Call Me on a Mission (169)

Hymn
+ Called to Serve (249)
+ Go Forth with Faith (263)

Gospel Art Book
+ Missionaries: Elders (109)
+ Missionaries: Sisters (110)

Scriptures
+ Matthew 28:19
+ D&C 115:5
+ Mark 16:15

Sharing the gospel helps others to come unto Christ.

Lesson

Jesus told His disciples, "Go ye therefore, and teach all nations, baptizing them in the name of the Father, and of the Son, and of the Holy Ghost" (Matthew 28:19). Many people have not had a chance to learn about Jesus Christ. It is our responsibility to share the gospel with them.

We do not have to serve a full-time mission in order to do missionary work. There are many things we can do to share the gospel. We can talk to our neighbors or our friends at school. We can invite someone to attend Primary or family home evening. Being a good example and standing up for our beliefs also helps others learn about the gospel. We should look for opportunities every day to share the gospel and help others come unto Christ.

Read and discuss John 21:15–17

+ Why did Jesus ask Simon Peter if he loved Him?
+ What did He mean when He said, "Feed my sheep"?

Activity

Younger Children: Draw a picture and mail it to a full-time missionary.
Older Children: Write a letter to a full-time missionary. Tell him or her what your family is doing to be member missionaries.

Challenge

Pray and ask Heavenly Father which of your friends or neighbors is ready to hear the missionary discussions. Then set a date with your family of when you would like to have them in your home to hear the discussions. Work on fellowshipping and preparing your friends to hear the gospel. Ask the ward mission leader to help you as needed.

Challenge

My family will invite

_____

to listen to the missionary discussions by this date:

_____.

Resources

(Select one from each category.)

Children's Songbook
+ Repentance (98)
+ Help Me, Dear Father (99)

Hymn
+ Come unto Jesus (117)
+ Come, Let Us Anew (217)
+ Lord, I Would Follow Thee (220)

Gospel Art Book
+ Enos Praying (72)

Scriptures
+ Isaiah 1:18
+ Matthew 4:17
+ 3 Nephi 9:22

We come unto Christ by repenting when we make a mistake.

Lesson

Enos was the son of Jacob, who was a Book of Mormon prophet. One day, Enos went into the woods to hunt. He started thinking about the things his father had taught him. Enos realized he did not always keep the commandments. He felt sorry for his sins and knelt down to pray. He prayed so long that the day turned into night.

Read and discuss Enos 1:4–8.
+ What did Enos mean when he said his "soul hungered"?
+ Why was Enos forgiven of his sins?

Read and discuss Enos 1:19–26.
+ Why did Enos preach repentance to the Nephites?
+ How can we share our testimonies of Jesus Christ with others?

Activity

All Ages: Watch a video of Enos's experience, available at https://www.lds.org/media-library/video/2010-12-11-chapter-11-enos?lang=eng.

Challenge

Sometime this week, read the parable of the prodigal son in Luke 15:11–32 and discuss the following with your family:

+ What was the turning point for the prodigal son?
+ How did his father react when he returned home? How did his brother react? Which man reacted the way Jesus would?

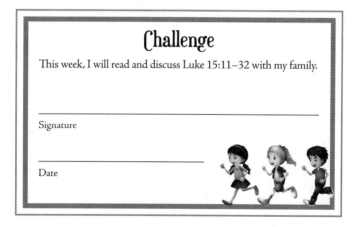

Challenge

This week, I will read and discuss Luke 15:11–32 with my family.

_____

Signature

_____

Date

Resources

(Select one from each category.)

Children's Songbook
+ I Love to See the Temple (95)
+ Families Can Be Together Forever (188)

Hymn
+ High on the Mountain Top (5)
+ We Love Thy House, O God (247)

Gospel Art Book
+ Salt Lake Temple (119)
+ Young Couple Going to the Temple (120)

Scriptures
+ Isaiah 2:2–3
+ D&C 2

Temple work helps me and my family come unto Christ.

Lesson

Many sacred ordinances take place in the temple. They include baptisms for the dead, endowments, and sealings. We must be worthy to enter the temple. We must obey the commandments and repent of our sins. When we go to the temple, we draw closer to Heavenly Father and Jesus Christ. We must receive the ordinances of the temple to live with them again.

Going to the temple helps us eternally, but it can also help us right now. Many fathers and mothers have said that attending the temple blesses their family. They are able to receive revelation on how to raise their children, and they feel greater peace and love in their home. Most important, temple work helps families draw closer to Jesus Christ.

Read and discuss Psalm 24:3–5.

+ What does it mean to have clean hands (besides washing them with soap and water)?
+ What are some of the blessings we receive from attending the temple? How does this help us come unto Christ?

Activity

All Ages, Option 1: If you live near a temple, take a walk along the temple grounds. Discuss the importance of the temple and talk about how you feel when you are at the temple.

All Ages, Option 2: Complete a four-generation chart on familysearch.org.

Challenge

Even though you are too young to enter the temple, you can prepare now to go there someday. It won't be long before you turn twelve and can perform baptisms for the dead. Choose one thing you will do now to prepare to go to the temple.

Challenge

In order to prepare to go to the temple, I will do the following:

_____

_____

_____

_____

November

When We Serve Others,
We Serve God

Resources

(Select one from each category.)

Children's Songbook
- I'm Trying to Be Like Jesus (78)
- Go the Second Mile (167)

Hymn
- A Poor Wayfaring Man of Grief (29)
- I'll Go Where You Want Me to Go (270)

Gospel Art Book
- The Ten Lepers (46)

Scriptures
- Matthew 7:12
- Ephesians 2:10
- D&C 64:33

Jesus Christ taught us how to serve others.

Lesson

Jesus spent His life serving others. He loved everyone, even the outcasts. One day, He went to a small town and met ten lepers. These men had sores all over their bodies. No one would help the lepers because everyone was afraid of getting the terrible disease.

But Jesus did not turn them away. When the lepers asked Him to heal them, He lovingly did so. Jesus told the lepers to go to the priests. On the way there, they were healed. But only one leper returned to thank Jesus.

We can learn two important lessons from this story. First, Jesus did not turn the lepers away. Even though others were afraid of them, Jesus listened to their problems and healed them. Second, Jesus did not expect anything in return. Though He was disappointed that only one leper thanked Him, He probably knew before He healed the lepers that not all of them would return. But He healed them anyway because He loved them and wanted them to be well. Jesus is the perfect example of how to love and serve others.

Read and discuss Matthew 5:16.

- ✦ What is the light that Jesus is speaking of?
- ✦ How can we let our lights shine?
- ✦ What can we do to follow Jesus's example and serve others?

Activity

Younger Children: Color the picture on page 120.
Older Children: See page 121.

Challenge

Sometimes the best way to serve people is to spend time with them. Find at least one person this week who needs your time and spend time uplifting him or her.

Challenge

This week, I commit to give some of my time to at least one person in need.

_____

Signature

_____

Date

Let your **light** so **shine** before men, that they may see your **good works**, and **glorify** your Father which is in heaven.

—Matthew 5:16

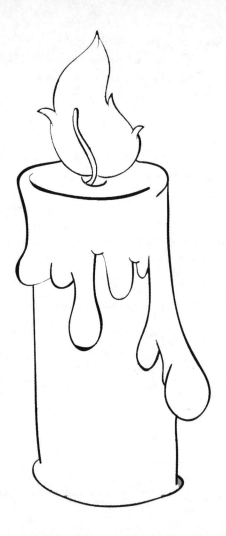

"Let your light so shine"

Unscramble the letters on each candle flame to reveal how we can let our lights shine, as Jesus taught in Matthew 5. *Solution on page 136.*

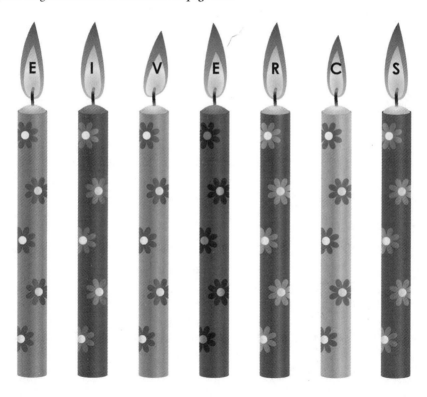

Resources

(Select one from each category.)

Children's Songbook
+ When We're Helping (198b)
+ "Give," Said the Little Stream (236)
+ I Have Two Little Hands (272)

Hymn
+ Because I Have Been Given Much (219)
+ You Can Make the Pathway Bright (228)

Scriptures
+ Mosiah 2:17
+ D&C 42:29

When I serve my family, I serve God.

Lesson

When Jesus was on the earth, He taught that those who will be saved at the last day are those who serve others. Let's read part of Matthew chapter 25 to find out what He said.

Read and discuss Matthew 25:34–40.
+ What did Jesus mean when He said, "Inasmuch as ye have done it unto one of the least of these my brethren, ye have done it unto me"?
+ How can we serve our family members?
+ How are we serving God when we serve each other?

In the Book of Mormon, King Benjamin teaches the same principle. Let's read what he said in the book of Mosiah.

Read and discuss Mosiah 2:17.
+ How is this scripture similar to the ones we read in Matthew 25?

Activity

All Ages: Do service project for a member of your extended family. If you don't live near your extended family, serve someone in your ward family.

Challenge

Sometimes the best types of service are anonymous acts. That means nobody except you and God know that you served someone. Choose a family member whom you wish to give a secret act of service this week. Fill out the challenge card. Keep it somewhere you will see it often, but make sure the other members of your family don't see it.

Challenge

This week, I will serve _____ by doing the following kind act:

_____

_____

_____

Week FOUR

Resources

(Select one from each category.)

Children's Songbook
- I'll Walk with You (140)
- A Happy Helper (197a)
- I Have Two Little Hands (272)

Hymn
- Scatter Sunshine (230)
- Let Us All Press On (243)

Gospel Art Book
- The Good Samaritan (44)

Scriptures
- Matthew 25:40
- Mosiah 2:17
- D&C 42:38

When I serve my neighbors, I serve God.

Lesson

Read and discuss the parable of the good Samaritan in Luke 10:25–37.

- According to the parable, who are our neighbors?
- How did the good Samaritan help his neighbor?
- How do we love our neighbors as ourselves? How can we serve them?

Activity

All Ages: As a family, do a service project for one of your neighbors.

Challenge

Part of serving God and our neighbors is showing love to everyone. This week, make a new friend by sitting by someone who is alone, playing with someone on the playground who doesn't have anyone to play with, or inviting someone you don't normally play with to come over to your house (with your parents' permission, of course).

Challenge

This week, I commit to make a new friend and treat him or her the way Jesus would.

_____

Signature

_____

Date

December

I Know That My Redeemer Lives

Resources

(Select one from each category.)

Children's Songbook
+ Samuel Tells of the Baby Jesus (36)
+ Once within a Lowly Stable (41)
+ Away in a Manger (42)

Hymn
+ Joy to the World (201)
+ O Little Town of Bethlehem (208)

Gospel Art Book
+ Joseph and Mary Travel to Bethlehem (29)
+ The Birth of Jesus (30)

Scriptures
+ Mosiah 3:8
+ Isaiah 9:6
+ 3 Nephi 11:10

Jesus Christ came to earth as promised by the prophets.

Lesson

Since the beginning of time, the prophets have taught that someday Jesus Christ would come to the earth to be our Savior. Isaiah, an Old Testament prophet, had many beautiful prophecies about the Savior. One of them is found in Isaiah 9: "For unto us a child is born, unto us a son is given: and the government shall be upon his shoulder: and his name shall be called Wonderful, Counsellor, The mighty God, The everlasting Father, The Prince of Peace" (v. 6).

The prophets taught that Jesus would be born a baby, just like the rest of us. But He would be different because He would have a special mission to fulfill. He would be the Savior of the world. He would make it possible for us to overcome sin and death and return to our Father in Heaven.

Read and discuss the birth of Jesus in Luke 2:1–19.

+ Why did the angel tell the shepherds not to fear?
+ Why was Jesus born in a manger?

Activity

All Ages, Option 1: Make Christmas cards to send to family and friends. Include your testimony of Jesus Christ.

All Ages, Option 2: Decorate your Christmas tree. Listen to Christ-centered Christmas music.

Challenge

It's nice to give people Christmas presents, but the most important part of Christmas is remembering the birth of Jesus Christ. This Christmas, give someone a gift centered around Jesus Christ that doesn't cost money. You could write them a letter with your testimony, make them a handmade gift, or do service for them.

Challenge

This Christmas I will give _____

a gift centered around Jesus Christ. I will give this person:

_____

_____

Signature

_____

Date

Week TWO

Resources

(Select one from each category.)

Children's Songbook
+ He Sent His Son (34)
+ Beautiful Savior (62)

Hymn
+ Redeemer of Israel (6)
+ How Great Thou Art (86)
+ The Lord Is My Shepherd (108)

Gospel Art Book
+ Jesus the Christ (1)
+ Mary and the Resurrected Jesus Christ (59)

Scriptures
+ 1 John 4:14
+ 1 John 2:2
+ D&C 43:34

Jesus Christ is the Savior of the world.

Lesson

During the Christmas season, it is easy to get caught up in all the parties, presents, and treats. But we must not forget Jesus Christ, the Savior of the world, who is the reason we celebrate Christmas.

On Christmas we give gifts to those we love. Jesus Christ gave all mankind a very special gift because He loves all of us so much. He gave each of us the chance to repent of our sins and live with Him and our Father in Heaven forever. This gift is not just limited to certain people. Everyone in the whole world can receive it if they choose to follow Him.

Not everyone has learned about Jesus Christ. But that does not mean they cannot receive His great gift. He has promised that every person who lives, or who ever has lived, on the earth will have a chance to accept Him as their Savior.

Read and discuss John 3:16.
+ Why did God give us His Son to be our Savior?
+ What does it mean to have everlasting life?

Activity

All Ages: Watch an uplifting Christmas movie. Make sure to choose a movie that portrays the true spirit of Christmas.

Challenge

Deliver a treat to a nonmember friend with a copy of "The Living Christ," written in the year 2000 by the First Presidency and the Quorum of the Twelve Apostles. You can obtain copies of "The Living Christ" through the Church Distribution Center, or you can print a copy at http://www.lds.org/languages/LivingChrist/LivingChristEnglish.pdf.

Challenge

I will deliver a treat with a copy of "The Living Christ" to the following person:

_____

_____
Signature

_____
Date

Jesus Christ will return to the earth someday.

Lesson

After Jesus was resurrected, He taught His disciples that even though He would soon return to His Father, He would come to earth again. But no one would know when that would be. Jesus said, "But of that day and hour knoweth no man, no, not the angels of heaven, but my Father only" (Matthew 24:36).

Latter-day prophets have taught that the Second Coming will take place soon. But we still do not know when that day will come. We need to live righteously and be ready to meet Jesus. It will be a glorious day for those who are prepared.

When Jesus comes again, He will establish His kingdom here on earth. We must be prepared for that day because only the righteous will remain on the earth. Even though we don't know exactly when Jesus will return, we have many scriptures that tell us which signs to look for.

Read and discuss Matthew 24. (It's a long chapter, so read it beforehand and select verses to read with your family.)

Resources

(Select one from each category.)

Children's Songbook
- When He Comes Again (82)
- The Tenth Article of Faith (128b)

Hymn
- The Spirit of God (2)
- Now Let Us Rejoice (3)

Gospel Art Book
- The Second Coming (66)

Scriptures
- 2 Thessalonians 1:7
- D&C 1:12
- D&C 43:29

- What are some of the signs of the Second Coming?
- How can we prepare for it?

Activity

All Ages: Bake Christmas cookies or another treat to deliver to your neighbors.

Challenge

This week, watch the news or read the newspaper with your parents and discuss some of the events that show the Second Coming is drawing near. However, remember the Savior's counsel in Matthew 24:6: "Be not troubled: for all these things must come to pass, but the end is not yet."

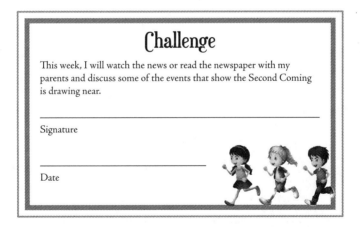

Challenge

This week, I will watch the news or read the newspaper with my parents and discuss some of the events that show the Second Coming is drawing near.

_____

Signature

_____

Date

Resources

(Select one from each category.)

Children's Songbook
- I Will Follow God's Plan (164)
- Families Can Be Together Forever (188)

Hymn
- O My Father (292)
- I Am a Child of God (301)
- Teach Me to Walk in the Light (304)

Scriptures
- John 3:14–15
- 2 Nephi 2:27
- 2 Nephi 9:39
- D&C 50:5

I can live with Jesus Christ again.

Lesson

Jesus Christ loves us very much. Through the Atonement, He made it possible for us to be resurrected and live with Him again someday. But we must do our part. We must have faith in Jesus Christ, repent of our sins, and keep the commandments. We must do all we can to follow His example and endure to the end.

Living with Jesus Christ and Heavenly Father again is called eternal life. They want to give this gift to us. In Moses 1:39, the Lord said, "For behold, this is my work and my glory—to bring to pass the immortality and eternal life of man." That means Heavenly Father and Jesus Christ are working very hard to help us make it back to them.

Do you remember when we learned about Enos? After he prayed all day and all night, he received forgiveness for his sins. When he grew older, he knew he would soon die. But he was not afraid because he knew he had lived a good life and would be with Jesus Christ and Heavenly Father again.

Read and discuss Enos 1:27.

+ Why wasn't Enos afraid to die?
+ What did he mean when he said he would rest in his Redeemer?
+ How can we have strong faith like Enos had?

Activity

All Ages: Celebrate the end of the year by playing your favorite family game and eating your favorite snack.

Challenge

Imagine that Jesus is living in your home. How would you behave? What would you do differently? Whenever you have to make a choice, pretend that Jesus is by your side. This will make it easier to choose the right.

Challenge

This week, I will live as if Jesus were in my home.

_____

Signature

_____

Date

Answer Key

PAGE 18

I KNOW THAT MY REDEE-MER LIVETH AND THAT HE SHALL STAND AT THE LAT-TER DAY UPON THE EARTH

PAGE 28

7. DALLIN H. OAKS
2. DIETER F. UCHTDORF
8. M. RUSSELL BALLARD
11. JEFFREY R. HOLLAND
13. QUENTIN L. COOK
10. ROBERT D. HALES
3. HENRY B. EYRING
5. L. TOM PERRY
14. D. TODD CHRISTOFFERSON
4. BOYD K. PACKER
9. RICHARD G. SCOTT
14. NEIL L. ANDERSEN
6. RUSSELL M. NELSON
1. THOMAS S. MONSON
12. DAVID A. BEDNAR

PAGE 34

PAGE 44

THE BOOK OF MORMON

PAGE 45

JOSEPH SMITH TRANSLATED THE BOOK OF MORMON.

PAGE 53

1. ORCHID
2. DAFFODIL
3. TULIP
4. ROSE
5. DAISY

HOPED

PAGE 58

PAGE 62

COVENANT

PAGE 67

THE FATHER HAS A BODY OF FLESH AND BONES AS TAN-GIBLE AS MAN'S; THE SON ALSO; BUT THE HOLY GHOST HAS NOT A BODY OF FLESH AND BONES, BUT IS A PERSO-NAGE OF SPIRIT. WERE IT NOT SO, THE HOLY GHOST COULD NOT DWELL IN US.
—D&C 130:22

PAGE 71

1. LOVE
2. JOY
3. PEACE
4. GENTLENESS
5. GOODNESS
6. FAITH

PAGE 91

PAGE 121

SERVICE

Fun Food for FHE

Simple, Kid-Friendly Recipes

These recipes may not be fancy, but they're simple, fun foods that children of all ages will enjoy making and eating.

S'mores Popcorn

¾ cup butter
2 (16-oz.) bags marshmallows
12 cups popped popcorn (remove unpopped kernels)
2 cups chocolate chips
1 cup graham crackers, broken into small pieces

1. Melt butter and marshmallows in a large saucepan.

2. Mix in popcorn. Let cool a few minutes.

3. When cool, stir in chocolate chips and graham cracker pieces. Mix with your hands, if necessary.

4. Press mixture firmly into a buttered cake pan.

Biscuit Donuts*

oil for deep frying
1 pkg. refrigerated biscuit dough
cinnamon and sugar, powdered sugar, or your favorite frosting

1. Fill a deep skillet with 2 inches of oil. Heat to 370 degrees.
2. Flatten dough to about ¼-inch thick. Use a tiny cup (such as a medicine cup) or another small round object to cut a hole in the center of the dough.
3. Fry each donut or donut hole for about 60 seconds on each side, or until golden brown.
4. Remove from oil and set on paper towels to drain excess oil.
5. Sprinkle with sugar or cover with frosting.

CAUTION: Deep frying can be very dangerous. A parent must help with this recipe.

Banana Bites

2 large bananas, sliced
½ cup peanut butter
chocolate chips

1. Lay banana slices on a plate or tray.
2. Spread ½ to 1 teaspoon peanut butter on each slice.
3. Top with chocolate chips.

Frozen Yogurt Drops

1 (8-oz.) carton yogurt (any flavor)
1 Ziploc bag

1. Fill Ziploc bag about halfway full of yogurt.
2. Cut one of the bottom corners of the Ziploc bag.
3. Pipe small dots of yogurt onto a pan.
4. Freeze for 1–2 hours.

Caramel Apple Dip

1 (8-oz.) pkg. cream cheese, softened
1 small jar marshmallow fluff
1 Tbsp. caramel sauce
1 small carton whipped topping

1. Combine cream cheese, marshmallow fluff, and caramel until smooth.
2. Fold in whipped topping.
3. Serve with apple slices.

Strawberry Sorbet

2 cups frozen strawberries
$1/3$ cup water
sugar to taste

1. Place all ingredients in the blender. To start, add 1–2 teaspoons sugar.

2. Blend until smooth.

3. Add more water, one tablespoon at a time, if the mixture is too thick; blend again until smooth.

4. Add more sugar if desired.

Hawaiian Coconut Pudding

1 can coconut milk
$^1/_3$ cup sugar
$^1/_3$ cup cornstarch
1 tsp. vanilla

1. Combine coconut milk and sugar in a saucepan.
2. Cook over medium heat, stirring frequently, until the mixture comes to a boil.
3. Add cornstarch gradually, stirring constantly.
4. Remove from heat and add vanilla.
5. Pour into a 8"x8" baking dish and refrigerate until firm.
6. Cut into 1-inch squares and enjoy.

Popsicles

8 (3-oz.) Dixie cups
2 cups juice of your choice
8 Popsicle sticks

Fill each cup $^2/_3$ full. Freeze for 15 minutes or until slushy enough that Popsicle sticks can stand up on their own. Insert one popsicle stick into each cup and freeze until hard. When ready to eat, peel paper cup away and enjoy.

Variation
To make a creamier Popsicle, use pureed fruit mixed with yogurt or milk.

Marshmallow Munchies

large marshmallows
Popsicle sticks or lollipop sticks
chocolate chips, melted*
shredded coconut, sprinkles, nuts, or crushed candy

1. Put a Popsicle or lollipop stick in each marshmallow.

2. Dip in melted chocolate.

3. Sprinkle with your topping of choice (shredded coconut, sprinkles, nuts, or crushed candy).

4. Refrigerate for a few minutes, or until chocolate hardens.

*How to Melt Chocolate Chips
1. Put chocolate chips in a microwave-safe bowl.
2. Microwave at 50 percent power for 1 minute. Remove from microwave and stir.
3. Continue to microwave in 30-second increments until chocolate is completely melted. Stir after each 30-second increment.

Easy Pudding Pie

1 pkg. pudding (the pie filling variety works best), made according
    to package directions
1 premade graham cracker crust
1 carton whipped topping

Mix pudding according to package instructions. Pour into graham cracker crust
and chill in refrigerator until firm. Spread whipped topping evenly over pie before
serving.

Variation
If using vanilla pudding, add a sliced banana or ½ cup shredded coconut.

Peanut Butter Candy

1½ cups peanut butter
$^1/_3$ cup powdered milk
$^1/_3$ cup honey

1. Mix together all ingredients.
2. Roll into 1-inch balls.
3. Keep refrigerated.

Notes

_____

_____

_____

_____

_____

_____

_____

_____

_____

_____

_____

Notes

_____

_____

_____

_____

_____

_____

_____

_____

_____

_____

_____